HIKING NORTH CAROLINA'S PISGAH RANGER DISTRICT

by Kirk Edwards

Published by Soco Publishing
Sylva, North Carolina

Hiking North Carolina's Pisgah Ranger District
by Kirk Edwards

Published by:
Soco Publishing
PO BOX 1021
Sylva, NC 28779-1021

Library of Congress Catalog Card Number 99-93612
ISBN   0-9668870-0-X

Cover photograph by Craig Litz
Cover design by Craig Litz
Author photograph by Bo Park
Other photographs by Kirk Edwards

Printed by Cherokee Boys Club
Manufactured in the USA

ACKNOWLEDGMENTS

A special thanks to the following individuals who devoted many hours to this project in order to produce a comprehensive manual: Tom Bodenheimer, Terry Clements, Gary Eblen, Charles Edwards, Kaye Edwards-Leigh, Laura McBane, Lane Nakaji, Bo Park, Brad Pejsa, Russ Robinette, Diane Smeltzer, and Roger Turner. Their assistance in the process of compiling information, proofreading, and hiking the trails was invaluable. It would not be what it is without them.

The U.S. Forest Service should also get a round of applause for providing a variety of helpful information.

USGS is another prime contributor for the use of the topographical maps that are included with each trail.

The author, Kirk Edwards, has hiked hundreds of miles in the mountains of North Carolina and is an enthusiast of many outdoor recreations including hiking, backpacking, mountain biking, and canoeing. His years of hiking experience made him realize what is needed in a good hiking guidebook. Therefore, he proceeded to develop one based on necessary trail information that is easy to understand and easy to use in the field. This guidebook will enhance your outdoor experience without spoiling the fun of exploring a new area.

For my dear family and friends.
Without their support and patience this would not
be possible.

CONTENTS

WARNING - DISCLAIMER

Every attempt has been made by the author and publisher to have the information in this book as accurate and complete as possible on the subject matter that it was intended to cover. However, there may be discrepancies in the content or errors of typographical nature. There are also the inevitable changes that will happen in the trails and the regulations concerning their use. Therefore, individuals using this book should use it as a general guide and should be aware that changes may have occurred since its publication. Individuals should also be aware that hiking and backcountry travel can be extremely strenuous and has certain risks that can be dangerous or even fatal.

The author and Soco Publishing accept no responsibility to any person for loss, damage, injury, or inconvenience caused or alleged, direct or indirect, from the information contained within.

Individuals who do not wish to be bound by the statement above should return the book to the publisher for an immediate full refund.

EMERGENCY NUMBERS

EMERGENCIES... DIAL 911

DISTRICT RANGER..............................(828) 877-3265

PARK WATCH.. (800) 727-5929

BUNCOMBE COUNTY.......................... (828) 255-5441

HAYWOOD COUNTY............................ (828) 452-2822

HENDERSON COUNTY........................ (828) 691-4911

TRANSYLVANIA COUNTY ....(828) 884-3168

> **District Ranger**
> **USDA Forest Service**
> **1001 Pisgah Hwy.**
> **Pisgah Forest, NC 28768**

REMINDERS

- Plan ahead by telling a friend or family member exactly where you are going and when you should return. Tell them when they should contact the authorities and who they should call. For the Pisgah Ranger District, contact the district office.
- Keep track of other members of your party and do not let them wander off.
- Be properly dressed and prepared for the weather.
- Know your limits.
- Practice and improve your skills using a compass and a map.

INTRODUCTION

The Pisgah Ranger District is located southwest of Asheville and north of Brevard and is easily accessible from several main roads including the Blue Ridge Parkway (see pages 18 and 19). The district ranger station is located on US 276 near Brevard and is open to the public 8:00 am to 5:00 pm Monday through Friday. They are also open on the weekends and holidays during the summer from 9:00 am to 5:00 pm.

The district covers over 150,000 acres; most of it was bought by the U.S. Forest Service from the Vanderbilt estate in 1914. This area was the first national forest east of the Mississippi River and today is the most visited national forest in North Carolina. Pisgah Ranger District is also the birthplace of forestry management in America and still serves as the location for the study of our woodlands.

There are hundreds of miles of trails, with different degrees of difficulty for any level of experience. These trails offer a vast array of outdoor activities, e.g. hiking, cycling, backpacking, horseback riding, rock climbing, fishing, wildlife observation, photography, and more. With so much to do it's no surprise why so many people come to the Pisgah Ranger District.

The peak season starts around mid-May and ends in early November, but due to the southern climate, most of the year is a good time to visit. Depending on timing, you may experience the lush hardwood forests of summer, the changing seasons in spring and fall, or wonderful winter views. No matter what your outdoor recreation might be, you will be enthralled by the seasonal beauty of the national forest!

The diversity of terrain offered in the area is amazing: Mountain peaks that brush the clouds at an elevation of over 6000 ft., rockfaces, open balds, and cascading waterfalls. Furthermore, various flora and fauna of the region are another attraction for many people. Natural wonders abound and give the outdoor enthusiast so many options to see. This diversity, immense area, and numerous trails bring people back year after year to the Pisgah Ranger District.

So get out, go hiking, and enjoy!

UNDERSTANDING THE BOOK

This book is to be used as a day hiking guide and should not be used for mountain biking, horseback riding, or camping. Most of the hikes listed have at least one trail that is devoted to hikers. A trail marker will designate the types of uses allowed on a specific trail. If a marker is not present then it is designated as hiking only.

Necessary Items: This section will give you a general idea of what should be brought with you on a day hike. However, the length of the hike, time of year, and the experience of the hiker will determine if other items will be necessary or if certain ones can be removed.

Wilderness Conduct: With a growing number of people interested in hiking and other outdoor activities, it has become necessary for all individuals to observe certain guidelines and low impact practices. This should add to your enjoyment of the outdoors and for others that follow.

Orientation: The orientation section gives you a general map of the region and of the Pisgah Ranger District. It should also be noted that for greater detail of the road system a road map, U.S. Forest Service trail map, *Trails Illustrated* map, or the *Delorme North Carolina Atlas and Gazetter* is extremely handy.

Regional Information: This section is an extra bonus by giving you information that will help in planning a trip or in finding the supplies you may need. This information is not a complete listing but it should get you started.

Hikes: Listed by the U.S. Forest Service name; however, you may be hiking on several different trails with different names to complete the hike.

Trail Head: Starting point for the hike. They are listed as a trail name or parking area where they start.

Trail Finish: Locating the end of the trail will give you an idea if it is necessary to drop a car at another location or if you will be returning to the same spot.

Hiking Distance: The combined distance of a series of trails or the distance out and back on a single trail.

Difficulty: A very subjective matter; however, a general term relative to the other trails listed in the book.

Time Allowance: An approximate idea of how long it would take an average hiker with a minimal number of rest stops to finish the hike. Note: Allow for some extra time to indulge in reasonable slothfulness, photography, and unexpected amazement.

Elevation Change: This is the total feet of all the uphills and gives a good idea of the difficulty of the hike.

USGS Map: The topography map or maps where the trail is located. These maps are produced by the U.S. Geological Survey, they are crucial for using with your compass and give you a larger view of the surrounding area.

Highlights: An idea of what you might see on the trail without depriving you of discovering some things on your own.

Trail Description: This is not a tree by tree description and should not be regarded as such. It will give you enough information about tricky areas so you will not spend most of an afternoon trying to figure out which way the trail went, but you must be diligent in following markers and using general common sense to find your way. Careful preparation for the trip will help eliminate problems later on.

Map: The maps are a visual representation of the description and should also be helpful in many ways from finding the trail head to helping you in the right direction. All maps contained in this book are oriented to true north.

Map Key: Explains the symbols listed on the maps.

NECESSARY ITEMS

This Book: It gives a description of the hike and a condensed map of the area.

Water: One liter per person minimum, hot weather or longer trails two liters minimum.

Food: The amount will depend on the trip but carry at least a snack in addition to having some emergency food.

Appropriate Clothing: The clothing to wear will depend on the time of year, altitude of the trail, and the weather forecast. As a general rule, plan for the worst, coldest, wettest day for that time of year and you can't go wrong. You may not want to wear all the clothing at the beginning of the hike but have it readily available. Other hiking and camping books have entire chapters devoted to this particular subject so refer to them for more information.

Flashlight, Spare Batteries & Bulb: In case you didn't realize it was a three hour hike and you only have two hours of daylight.

First Aid Kit: Should contain assorted bandages, antiseptic, butterfly strips, ace bandage, moleskin, space blanket, ibuprofen, personal medications, minimum! It should also be noted that a course in first-aid from the American Red Cross or other certified organization would be a must for any backcountry traveler.

Whistle: Can be heard over loud noises such as running water and you can blow a whistle almost indefinitely.

Knife/Multi-tool: For assorted uses. Preferably lightweight, no machetes, please.

Topographic Map: A larger view of the area, better than a guidebook map and necessary for use with your compass.

Compass: To keep you from getting lost. However, owning one does not mean you know how to use it. Purchase a book on map and compass, and in an afternoon you will have the basic knowledge that has guided travelers throughout the centuries.

Matches or Lighter: To start a fire if you get caught out at night.

Fire Starter or Candle: Convenient way to start a fire and have some light especially in wet conditions.

Iodine Tablets: Purifies water and prevents you from spending a few days in the hospital after drinking contaminated water. Do not use if you are allergic to iodine; purchase a quality backpacking water filter instead.

Rain Jacket & Hat: Expect it to rain every time you go out, so be prepared. Rain gear will also help keep you warm if it gets cold and windy.

Quality Hiking Boots and Socks: Purchase boots that are comfortable and give you proper support. Your local retailer can show you options and answer questions on the subject.

Sunscreen & Insect Repellent: Compact quanities; you don't need a gallon for a day hike.

Toilet paper, Trowel & Sealable Plastic Bags: This allows you to do what is most natural in the wilderness without making an unsightly mess on yourself or the backcountry.

Watch: By knowing when it gets dark you can track how much daylight you have left. Furthermore, keep track of your progress by knowing how far you've gone and the distance remaining.

Sunglasses: To keep debris, bugs, the sun, (as well as the limb your hiking partner forgot to hold out of the way), from getting in your eyes.

Some Cash: $5 or $10 in cash and a dollar in change will suffice for emergencies.

Extra Car Keys: In the off-chance that you fall in the creek and your primary set of keys get swept downstream. You don't even have to carry them with you. Attach them somewhere under your car in a magnetic box.

Daypack or Fanny Pack: It makes a convenient way to carry all this stuff. Note: Things that you do not want to spill or leak, pack in resealable plastic bags.

Other Items not necessary but nice to have: Walking stick, camera, binoculars, altimeter, GPS, book, notepad and pencil.

PROPER WILDERNESS CONDUCT

General Reflection

Today our wilderness experience is very different from what it was even twenty years ago. More and more people are enjoying our natural areas in many different ways; unfortunately there has been very little expansion of these areas to create new trails for these additional outdoor enthusiasts. Therefore, rules and regulations have been created to protect our natural resources. A set of general rules have been developed to keep the national forest in a pristine condition for everyone to enjoy. Following the basics shouldn't take away from your own outdoor experience, in fact it should foster a type of husbandry with our national forest. If you enjoy the wilderness, why do anything that would cause harm to it?

Hiking

Stay on the designated trail and walk single file. Mud holes and other obstacles should be crossed rather than skirted; it will only cause the trail to be widened or lead to the development of several trails.

Try to stay on the most durable substance: Rock, sand, or dirt as opposed to roots or vegetation.

Keep hiking groups to a minimum number.

Hike during off seasons and times to reduce impact. It will also enhance your own enjoyment.

Pack out anything that you have brought in and help by picking up someone else's carelessly discarded trash.

Do not cut switchbacks; it will save you very little time and will cause erosion.

Keep loud noises to a minimum; it disturbs people and wildlife.

Leave any natural objects or artifacts where you find them for others to enjoy. Someone else has probably left the ones that you will find.

Avoid brightly colored clothing except during hunting season when a blaze orange vest is a necessity. Contact the ranger station or the North Carolina Wildlife Resources Commission for hunting season dates.

Human Waste
When nature calls on a hike you should be aware of the correct practice of disposal to avoid contaminating nearby water sources or leaving it out for everyone to see. Human waste should be buried in a "cathole" that is at least six inches deep, about the width of this book closed, and at least two hundred feet from water sources, campsites, and trails. Toilet paper should at least be buried if not packed out in a plastic zip type closure bag.

Dogs
The Pisgah Ranger District does allow dogs but they must be leashed and under control. Please remove any feces from the trail or pack it out.

Sharing The Trail
Most of the trails listed in this book have at least one section of trail designated for hikers only. However, getting to them or making them into a loop hike requires sharing the trail with people on bikes and on horseback.

Hikers must yield to horses. Step off the trail, preferably downhill. Quietly listen for any instructions the rider may give you and don't make sudden movements. If hiking with your dog keep it under control and don't allow it to scare the horses.

Mountain bikers should yield to hikers, but on trails where bikes are allowed, listen for approaching riders and allow ample room for them to pass.

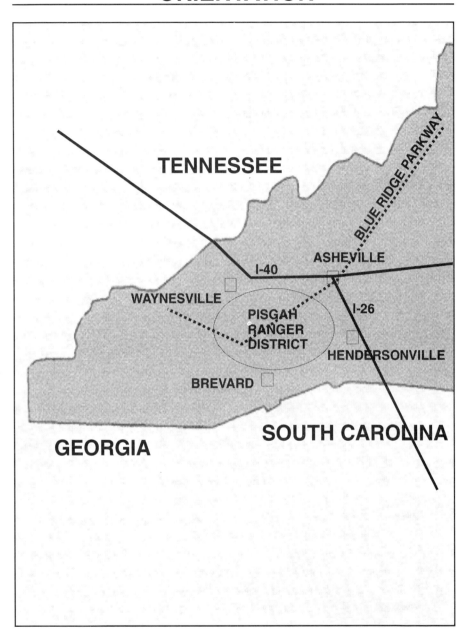

WESTERN NORTH CAROLINA

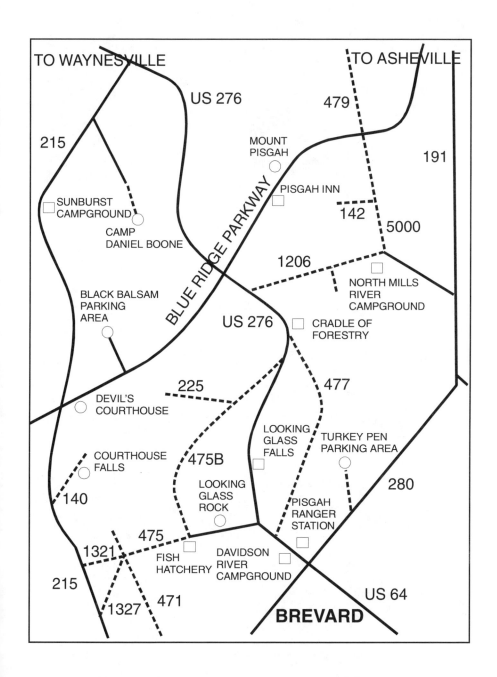

PISGAH RANGER DISTRICT AREA

PINK BEDS TRAIL

EASY HIKES

ANDY COVE
COURTHOUSE FALLS
GRAVEYARD FIELDS
MOORE COVE
PINK BEDS
CEMETERY LOOP
LITTLE SAM
SAM KNOB
BEAR BRANCH

ANDY COVE

TRAILHEAD:	PISGAH RANGER STATION
TRAIL FINISH:	PISGAH RANGER STATION
BLAZE COLOR:	NONE
HIKING DISTANCE:	2.2 MILES
DIFFICULTY:	EASY
TIME ALLOWANCE:	50 MINUTES
ELEVATION CHANGE:	100 FT.
USGS MAP:	PISGAH FOREST

HIGHLIGHTS:

Several bridged creek crossings, one swinging bridge, labeled examples of wildlife, and a beautiful walk next to the Davidson River.

TRAIL DESCRIPTION:

- Trail begins directly behind the ranger station parking area with a sign marked Andy Cove Nature Trail.
- .6 mile sharp right turn on unmarked Exercise Trail. Caution: Heavy traffic on US 276.
- Left turn after bridge and go through the English Chapel parking area.
- Left turn across the next bridge.
- Left turn onto the gravel road after the bridge.
- Short distance and the trail breaks off the gravel road into the woods on the right.
- Follow this back to the ranger station. Caution: Heavy traffic on US 276.

PACK IT IN , PACK IT OUT.

TRAIL MAP

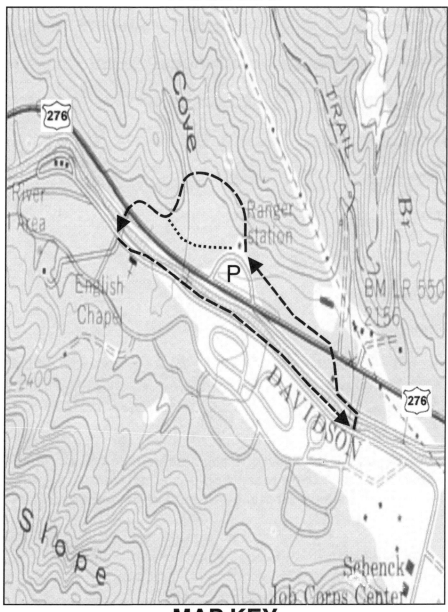

MAP KEY

FEATURED HIKE	- - - -►	US ROUTE	
OTHER TRAILS	··············	STATE ROUTE	
PARKING	P	FOREST ROAD	
WATERFALLS	W	GATE	●—●

STAY ON THE TRAIL. DO NOT CUT SWITCHBACKS.

COURTHOUSE FALLS

TRAILHEAD:	COURTHOUSE FALLS PARKING
TRAIL FINISH:	COURTHOUSE FALLS PARKING
BLAZE COLOR:	ORANGE
HIKING DISTANCE:	0.7 MILE
DIFFICULTY:	EASY
TIME ALLOWANCE:	45 MINUTES
ELEVATION CHANGE:	80 FT.
USGS MAP:	SAM KNOB

HIGHLIGHTS:

A leisurely hike next to the creek with a beautiful cascading waterfall at the end.

TRAIL DESCRIPTION:

- Courthouse Falls parking area is located almost at the end of forest road 140 on the far side of a small bridge. From the Blue Ridge Parkway take 215 toward Rosman and 140 will be the first left.

- Trail begins across the road from the parking area. Marked Courthouse Falls and Summey Cove.

- .3 mile sharp turn to the left marked Courthouse Falls. Caution: Waterfalls can be dangerous.

- Follow trail back to the parking area.

PACK IT IN , PACK IT OUT.

TRAIL MAP

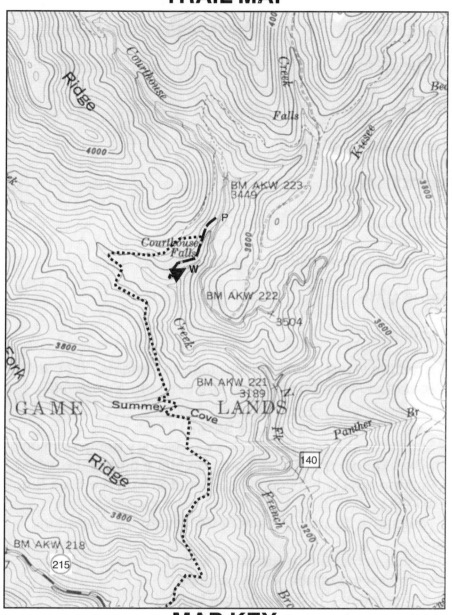

MAP KEY

FEATURED HIKE	- - - →	**US ROUTE**
OTHER TRAILS	··············	**STATE ROUTE**
PARKING	**P**	**FOREST ROAD**
WATERFALLS	**W**	**GATE**

STAY ON THE TRAIL. DO NOT CUT SWITCHBACKS.

GRAVEYARD FIELDS

TRAILHEAD:	GRAVEYARD FIELDS PARKING
TRAIL FINISH:	GRAVEYARD FIELDS PARKING
BLAZE COLOR:	BLUE
HIKING DISTANCE:	3 MILES
DIFFICULTY:	EASY
TIME ALLOWANCE:	2 HOURS
ELEVATION CHANGE:	150 FT.
USGS MAP:	SHINING ROCK

HIGHLIGHTS:

Incredible views of the surrounding mountains. Interesting vegetation in the open fields, streams, and a waterfall.

TRAIL DESCRIPTION:
- Suggestion: Graveyard Fields can be very congested on the weekends; try this trail out sometime during the week.
- Parking area is between US 276 and 215 on the Blue Ridge Parkway.
- Trail starts directly in back of Graveyard Fields parking area.
- Almost immediately, the other end of Graveyard Fields trail intersects on the left, go straight.
- .2 mile cross a bridge and turn to the left.
- .8 mile trail intersects to the left, go straight.
- 1.6 miles trail ends at the upper falls. Caution: Waterfalls can be dangerous.
- Turn back the way you came until reaching the intersection of the trail on the right.
- Follow this trail back to the parking area.

PACK IT IN , PACK IT OUT.

TRAIL MAP

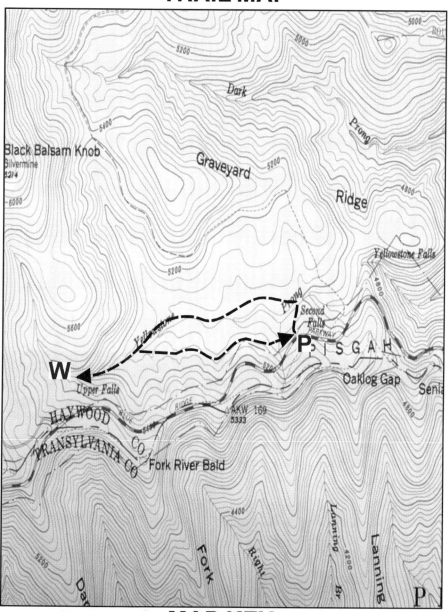

MAP KEY

FEATURED HIKE	- - - - ▶	**US ROUTE**	⬡
OTHER TRAILS	··············	**STATE ROUTE**	◯
PARKING	**P**	**FOREST ROAD**	▭
WATERFALLS	**W**	**GATE**	•━•

STAY ON THE TRAIL. DO NOT CUT SWITCHBACKS.

MOORE COVE

TRAILHEAD:	MOORE COVE PARKING AREA
TRAIL FINISH:	MOORE COVE PARKING AREA
BLAZE COLOR:	YELLOW
HIKING DISTANCE:	1.6 MILES
DIFFICULTY:	EASY
TIME ALLOWANCE:	1 HOUR
ELEVATION CHANGE:	150 FT.
USGS MAP:	SHINING ROCK

HIGHLIGHTS:

Several bridged creek crossings, an open hardwood forest, and a rock amphitheater with a free falling waterfall.

TRAIL DESCRIPTION:

- Parking area is approximately halfway between Looking Glass Falls and Sliding Rock Recreation Area on US 276.

- Trail starts across a bridge at the upper end of the parking area.

- Follow yellow trail blazes.

- .8 mile trail ends at the waterfall. Caution: Waterfalls can be dangerous.

- Follow trail back to parking area.

PACK IT IN , PACK IT OUT.

TRAIL MAP

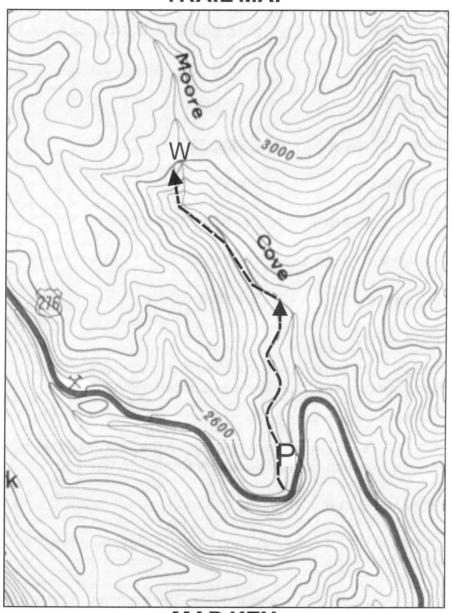

MAP KEY

FEATURED HIKE	----➤	US ROUTE	
OTHER TRAILS	··············	STATE ROUTE	
PARKING	**P**	FOREST ROAD	
WATERFALLS	**W**	GATE	

STAY ON THE TRAIL. DO NOT CUT SWITCHBACKS.

PINK BEDS

TRAILHEAD:	**PINK BEDS PARKING AREA**
TRAIL FINISH:	**PINK BEDS PARKING AREA**
BLAZE COLOR:	**ORANGE**
HIKING DISTANCE:	**2.2 MILES**
DIFFICULTY:	**EASY**
TIME ALLOWANCE:	**1 HOUR 30 MINUTES**
ELEVATION CHANGE:	**100 FT.**
USGS MAP:	**SHINING ROCK**

HIGHLIGHTS:

Bridged creek crossings, rhododendron tunnels, open fields, and a variety of flora throughout the hike.

TRAIL DESCRIPTION:

- Pink Beds parking area is just above the Cradle of Forestry in America Forest Discovery Center on US 276.

- Trail starts to the left of the field on a gravel road.

- After the first creek crossing the trail splits, take the left fork.

- 1.0 mile the Mountains to the Sea Trail crosses. Take this trail to the right.

- 1.2 miles the other side of the Pink Beds Loop crosses the trail. Take this trail to the right.

- Trail meets back at the split, left turn.

PACK IT IN , PACK IT OUT.

TRAIL MAP

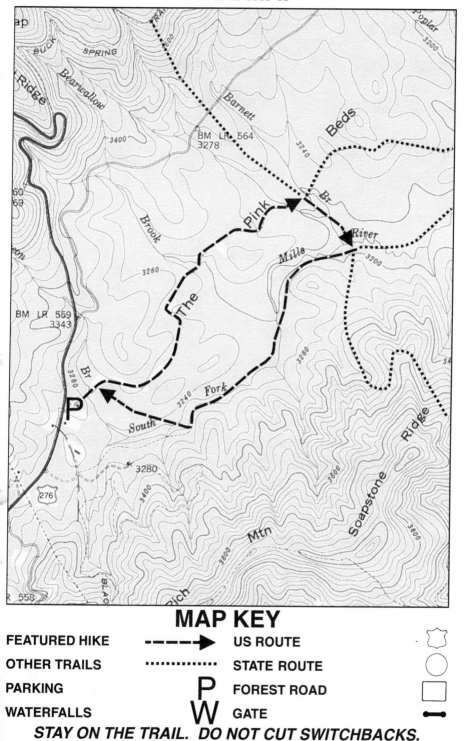

MAP KEY

FEATURED HIKE	– – – ➤	**US ROUTE**
OTHER TRAILS	··········	**STATE ROUTE**
PARKING	**P**	**FOREST ROAD**
WATERFALLS	**W**	**GATE**

STAY ON THE TRAIL. DO NOT CUT SWITCHBACKS.

CEMETERY LOOP

TRAILHEAD:	LONG BRANCH PARKING AREA
TRAIL FINISH:	LONG BRANCH PARKING AREA
BLAZE COLOR:	YELLOW
HIKING DISTANCE:	1.8 MILES
DIFFICULTY:	EASY
TIME ALLOWANCE:	1 HOUR 15 MINUTES
ELEVATION CHANGE:	130 FT.
USGS MAP:	SHINING ROCK

HIGHLIGHTS:

A great hike through rhododendron and mountain laurel. Please stay on the trail to avoid damage to the cemetery.

TRAIL DESCRIPTION:
- The parking area is located on forest road 475 near Gloucester Gap with a sign for Long Branch Trail and McCall Cemetery.

- .7 mile Cemetery Loop breaks off Long Branch, orange blazes. Continue up the hill on Cemetery Loop, yellow blazes.

- .9 mile trail connects with an old road, turn left.

- 1.2 miles trail connects with a new road, turn left.

- 1.8 miles the trail ends on forest road 475, turn left to the parking area.

PACK IT IN , PACK IT OUT.

TRAIL MAP

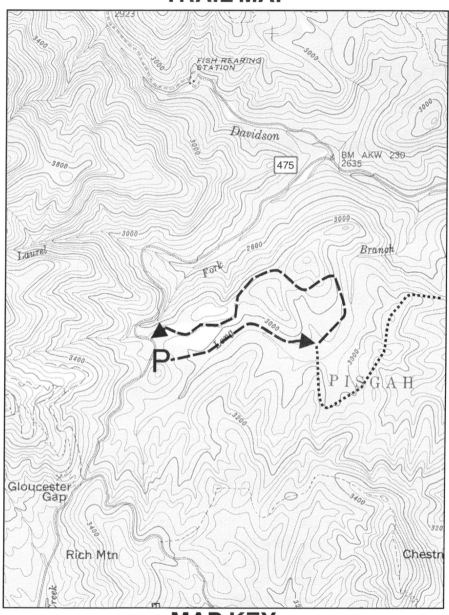

MAP KEY

FEATURED HIKE	– – – –▶	US ROUTE
OTHER TRAILS	·············	STATE ROUTE
PARKING	**P**	FOREST ROAD
WATERFALLS	**W**	GATE

STAY ON THE TRAIL. DO NOT CUT SWITCHBACKS.

LITTLE SAM

TRAILHEAD:	BLACK BALSAM PARKING AREA
TRAIL FINISH:	BLACK BALSAM PARKING AREA
BLAZE COLOR:	YELLOW
HIKING DISTANCE:	4 MILES
DIFFICULTY:	EASY
TIME ALLOWANCE:	2 HOURS 45 MINUTES
ELEVATION CHANGE:	600 FT.
USGS MAP:	SAM KNOB

HIGHLIGHTS:

Views, views, views. Don't forget your camera!

TRAIL DESCRIPTION:

- The trail head starts at Black Balsam parking area on Black Balsam road off the Blue Ridge Parkway.
- At the far end of the parking area you will find the trail marked Flat Laurel Creek; it's an old road bed.
- .9 mile follow Little Sam to the left.
- 1.2 miles a confusing right turn with a sign for Little Sam. Turn right. A few tricky sections.
- 2.0 miles Little Sam ends on the Mountains To Sea Trail, white blazes. Turn left.
- 2.7 miles Art Loeb is on your right. Go straight.
- 3.5 miles intersect with the Black Balsam road, turn left. Caution: Motor vehicle traffic.
- Follow the road back to the parking area.

PACK IT IN , PACK IT OUT.

TRAIL MAP

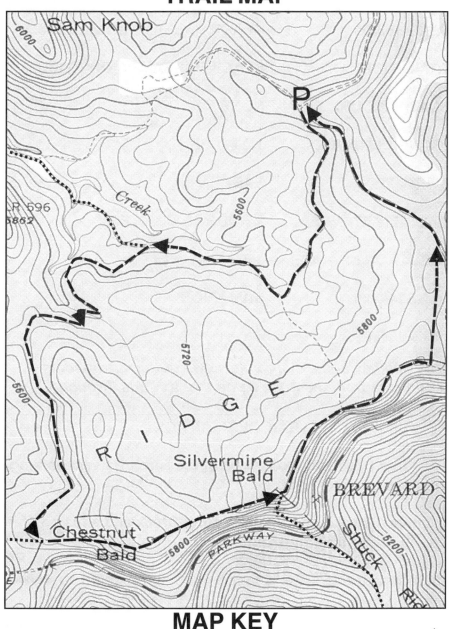

MAP KEY

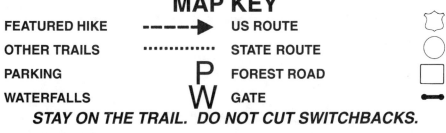

FEATURED HIKE	- - - -▶	US ROUTE
OTHER TRAILS	·············	STATE ROUTE
PARKING	P	FOREST ROAD
WATERFALLS	W	GATE

STAY ON THE TRAIL. DO NOT CUT SWITCHBACKS.

SAM KNOB

TRAILHEAD:	**BLACK BALSAM PARKING AREA**
TRAIL FINISH:	**BLACK BALSAM PARKING AREA**
BLAZE COLOR:	**NONE**
HIKING DISTANCE:	**1.9 MILES**
DIFFICULTY:	**EASY**
TIME ALLOWANCE:	**1 HOUR 15 MINUTES**
ELEVATION CHANGE:	**360 FT.**
USGS MAP:	**SAM KNOB**

HIGHLIGHTS:

This trail has some incredible views of the surrounding mountains from the open fields that it winds through.

TRAIL DESCRIPTION:

- The trail begins at the far end of the Black Balsam parking area marked Sam Knob.

- .5 mile the trail crosses Flat Laurel Creek and ends on Flat Laurel Creek Trail, turn left.

- .7 mile Little Sam starts to the right. Keep going straight on Flat Laurel Creek.

- Follow this back up the mountain to the parking area.

PACK IT IN , PACK IT OUT.

TRAIL MAP

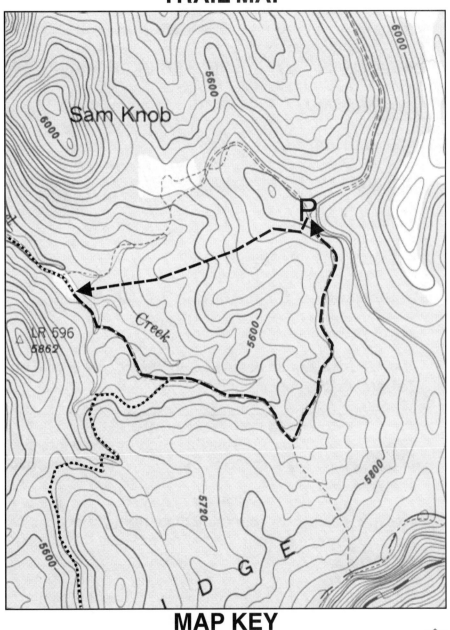

MAP KEY

FEATURED HIKE	- - - - →	US ROUTE
OTHER TRAILS	·············	STATE ROUTE
PARKING	P	FOREST ROAD
WATERFALLS	W	GATE

STAY ON THE TRAIL. DO NOT CUT SWITCHBACKS.

BEAR BRANCH

TRAILHEAD:	BEAR BRANCH PARKING AREA
TRAIL FINISH:	BEAR BRANCH PARKING AREA
BLAZE COLOR:	BLUE
HIKING DISTANCE:	2.5 MILES
DIFFICULTY:	EASY
TIME ALLOWANCE:	1 HOUR
ELEVATION CHANGE:	120 FT.
USGS MAP:	DUNSMORE MOUNTAIN

HIGHLIGHTS:

Bear Branch has an easy hike up the mountain with open forests, fields, and streams.

TRAIL DESCRIPTION:
- The trail head starts across the road from the intersection of forest road 142 and forest road 5000. 142 is the road to Trace Ridge.

- Keep the fields on your immediate right. There is a sign for Bear Branch to your left but do not take that route, keep straight.

- Turn left onto an old logging road. Several logging roads will intersect, stay on the main logging road.

- Trail intersects with forest road 5000, turn left. Caution: Motor vehicle traffic.

- 2.5 miles parking area

PACK IT IN , PACK IT OUT.

TRAIL MAP

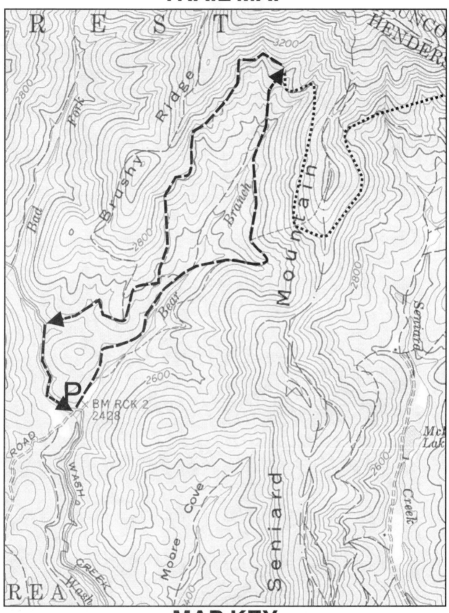

MAP KEY

FEATURED HIKE	- - - - ▶	**US ROUTE**
OTHER TRAILS	··············	**STATE ROUTE**
PARKING	**P**	**FOREST ROAD**
WATERFALLS	**W**	**GATE**

STAY ON THE TRAIL. DO NOT CUT SWITCHBACKS.

Coontree Loop Trail

MODERATE HIKES

COONTREE LOOP
BUCK SPRING
JOHN ROCK
LOOKING GLASS ROCK
MOUNT PISGAH
SLICK ROCK FALLS
SUNWALL
DANIEL RIDGE LOOP
PILOT COVE

COONTREE LOOP

TRAILHEAD:	COONTREE PICNIC AREA
TRAIL FINISH:	COONTREE PICNIC AREA
BLAZE COLOR:	BLUE
HIKING DISTANCE:	3.7 MILES
DIFFICULTY:	MODERATE
TIME ALLOWANCE:	2 HOURS
ELEVATION CHANGE:	970 FT.
USGS MAP:	SHINING ROCK

HIGHLIGHTS:

Ridge top hiking, tall stands of hardwoods, and some creeks. Best enjoyed in the fall for the views.

TRAIL DESCRIPTION:

- Coontree picnic area is located on US 276 and is well marked.
- The trail starts on the other side of US 276 from the parking area, blue blazes. Caution: Heavy traffic on US 276.
- .2 miles the trail forks, take the trail to the right.
- At the ridge Coontree Loop joins with Bennett Gap Trail, red blazes. Turn left onto this trail.
- In approximately .5 mile Coontree Loop breaks off Bennett Gap to the left. Follow Coontree Loop to the bottom of the mountain.
- The trail meets back at the fork; follow it to the picnic area.

PACK IT IN , PACK IT OUT.

TRAIL MAP

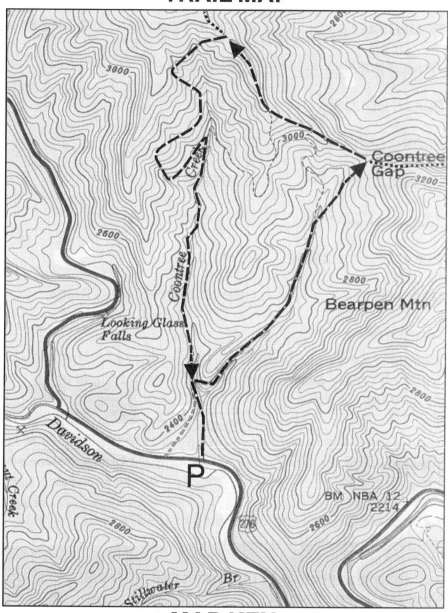

MAP KEY

FEATURED HIKE	----→	US ROUTE
OTHER TRAILS	···········	STATE ROUTE
PARKING	P	FOREST ROAD
WATERFALLS	W	GATE

STAY ON THE TRAIL. DO NOT CUT SWITCHBACKS.

BUCK SPRING

TRAILHEAD:	BUCK SPRING PARKING AREA
TRAIL FINISH:	PISGAH INN
BLAZE COLOR:	WHITE
HIKING DISTANCE:	5.3 MILES
DIFFICULTY:	MODERATE
TIME ALLOWANCE:	3 HOURS 30 MINUTES
ELEVATION CHANGE:	1300 FT.
USGS MAP:	CRUSO AND SHINING ROCK

HIGHLIGHTS:

Beautiful views of the surrounding area. Well maintained trail that crosses several creeks and a great finale at the Pisgah Inn.

TRAIL DESCRIPTION:

Suggestion: When dropping off your car at the Pisgah Inn, please ask at the front desk where you should leave your car.

- The trail starts on the upper end of US 276 near the Blue Ridge Parkway at the Buck Spring parking area.

- .5 miles intersection of the Mountains To The Sea Trail on your left, keep straight.

- .8 mile the Mountains To The Sea Alternative Route on the right, stay straight.

- Some steep sections near the end. Continue on the trail back to the Pisgah Inn.

PACK IT IN , PACK IT OUT.

TRAIL MAP

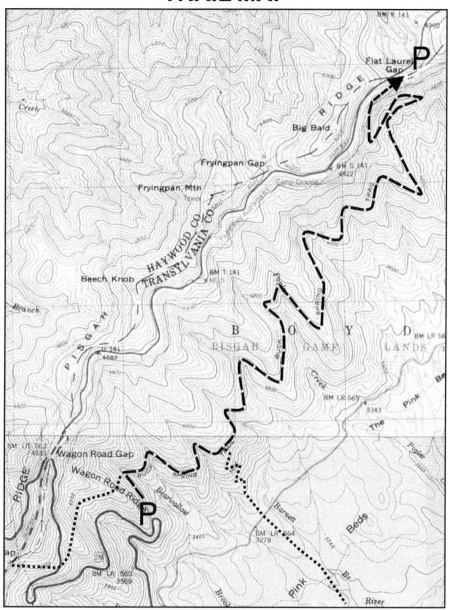

MAP KEY

FEATURED HIKE	- - - ▶	US ROUTE
OTHER TRAILS	··············	STATE ROUTE
PARKING	P	FOREST ROAD
WATERFALLS	W	GATE

STAY ON THE TRAIL. DO NOT CUT SWITCHBACKS.

JOHN ROCK

TRAILHEAD:	FISH HATCHERY PARKING
TRAIL FINISH:	FISH HATCHERY PARKING
BLAZE COLOR:	YELLOW
HIKING DISTANCE:	5 MILES
DIFFICULTY:	MODERATE
TIME ALLOWANCE:	2 HOURS 45 MINUTES
ELEVATION CHANGE:	1200 FT.
USGS MAP:	SHINING ROCK

HIGHLIGHTS:

Spectacular views from John Rock of Looking Glass Rock and the Parkway.

TRAIL DESCRIPTION:

- The Fish Hatchery is located at the end of the pavement on 475 coming from the 276 side.
- Cat Gap Loop trail is located at the end of the parking area, orange blazes.
- Follow the blazes up the mountain.
- John Rock on the right, yellow blazes, turn here.
- At the top, the trail runs out on the face of John Rock. Caution: Rock cliffs can be dangerous.
- Take a right back on the trail, very steep sections.
- Turn right on Cat Gap Bypass, follow this trail.
- Turn right onto Cat Gap Loop, down the mountain.
- Butter Gap on left; continue straight on Cat Gap Loop.
- Turn left on service road and follow this to parking area.

PACK IT IN , PACK IT OUT.

TRAIL MAP

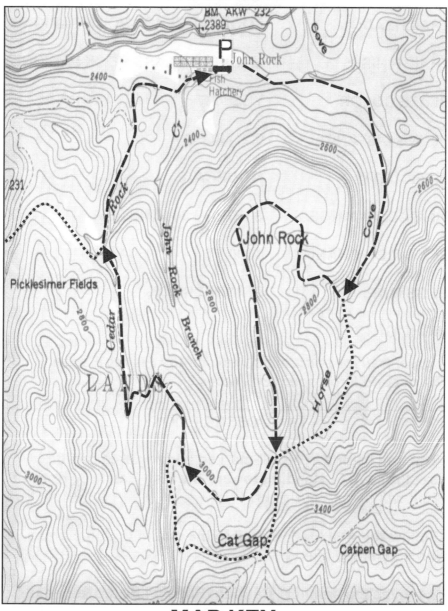

MAP KEY

FEATURED HIKE	----▶	US ROUTE
OTHER TRAILS	··········	STATE ROUTE
PARKING	P	FOREST ROAD
WATERFALLS	W	GATE

STAY ON THE TRAIL. DO NOT CUT SWITCHBACKS.

LOOKING GLASS ROCK

TRAILHEAD:	LOOKING GLASS ROCK PARKING
TRAIL FINISH:	LOOKING GLASS ROCK PARKING
BLAZE COLOR:	YELLOW
HIKING DISTANCE:	6.2 MILES
DIFFICULTY:	MODERATE
TIME ALLOWANCE:	3 HOURS 30 MINUTES
ELEVATION CHANGE:	1600 FT.
USGS MAP:	SHINING ROCK

HIGHLIGHTS:

A great trail for panoramic views of the Pisgah Ranger District and large open rock faces.

TRAIL DESCRIPTION:

- The trail begins in a well-marked parking area beside forest road 475. Heading toward the Fish Hatchery from US 276 it will be on your right.

- Follow the well marked trail to the summit. Some areas with very steep hiking.

- 3.1 miles the summit. Caution: Sheer cliffs are very dangerous.

- Return to the parking area back down the same trail you came up.

PACK IT IN , PACK IT OUT.

TRAIL MAP

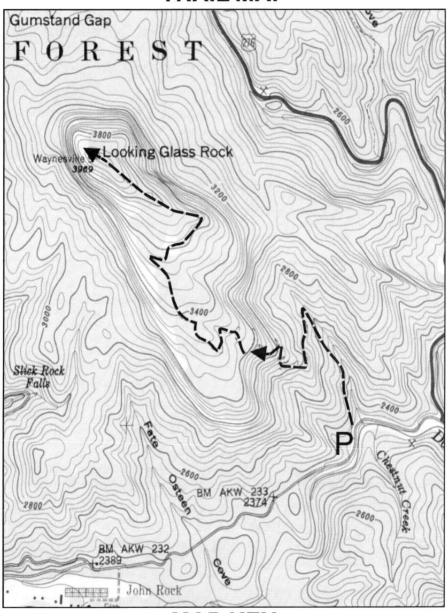

Gumstand Gap

F O R E S T

Looking Glass Rock

Waynesville
3969

Slick Rock
Falls

Fate Osteen

BM AKW 233
2374

BM AKW 232
2389

John Rock

P

Chestnut Creek

Cove

MAP KEY

FEATURED HIKE ------►   **US ROUTE**

OTHER TRAILS ············   **STATE ROUTE**

PARKING   P   **FOREST ROAD**

WATERFALLS   W   **GATE**

STAY ON THE TRAIL. DO NOT CUT SWITCHBACKS.

MOUNT PISGAH

TRAILHEAD:	MOUNT PISGAH PARKING AREA
TRAIL FINISH:	MOUNT PISGAH PARKING AREA
BLAZE COLOR:	NONE
HIKING DISTANCE:	2.6 MILES
DIFFICULTY:	MODERATE
TIME ALLOWANCE:	1 HOUR 45 MINUTES
ELEVATION CHANGE:	720 FT.
USGS MAP:	CRUSO AND DUNSMORE MOUNTAIN
HIGHLIGHTS:	

Stunning panoramic views of the entire Swannanoa Valley and on clear days, a view all the way to Mount Mitchell.

TRAIL DESCRIPTION:

- Road to the parking area is located between the Pisgah Inn and Buck Spring Tunnel.

- Start from the second parking area next to the sign for Mount Pisgah.

- 1.3 miles to the top of the observation platform and on top of the world. Be aware that there are some very steep sectons of this trail. Take your time.

- Return to the parking area back down the same trail.

PACK IT IN , PACK IT OUT.

TRAIL MAP

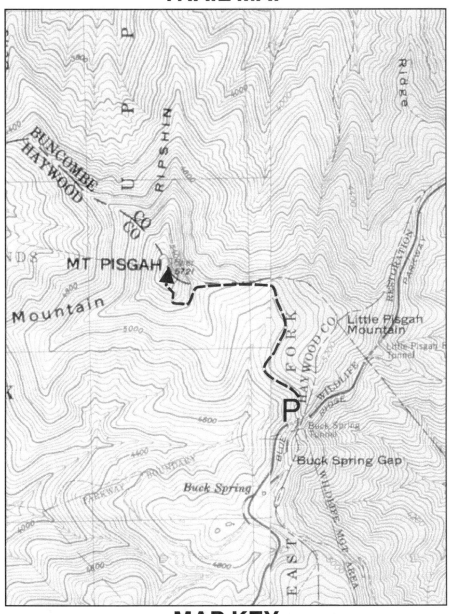

MAP KEY

FEATURED HIKE	- - - - ➤	US ROUTE
OTHER TRAILS	·············	STATE ROUTE
PARKING	**P**	FOREST ROAD
WATERFALLS	**W**	GATE

STAY ON THE TRAIL. DO NOT CUT SWITCHBACKS.

SLICK ROCK FALLS

TRAILHEAD:	SLICK ROCK FALLS PARKING
TRAIL FINISH:	SLICK ROCK FALLS PARKING
BLAZE COLOR:	YELLOW
HIKING DISTANCE:	1.8 MILES
DIFFICULTY:	MODERATE
TIME ALLOWANCE:	1 HOUR 30 MINUTES
ELEVATION CHANGE:	600 FT.
USGS MAP:	SHINING ROCK

HIGHLIGHTS:

The trail winds up the mountain past Slick Rock Falls across bridged stream crossings to the base of Looking Glass Rock.

TRAIL DESCRIPTION:

- The parking area is located on forest road 475B and is well marked.

- The trail runs up the hill past an information board and was being rerouted at the time this was written. However, the trail is well marked and after the new work it should be even better.

- Follow the trail to the base of Looking Glass Rock. Caution: Rock climbers use this area so be aware and stay well out of their way.

- Proceed back down the trail to the parking area.

PACK IT IN , PACK IT OUT.

TRAIL MAP

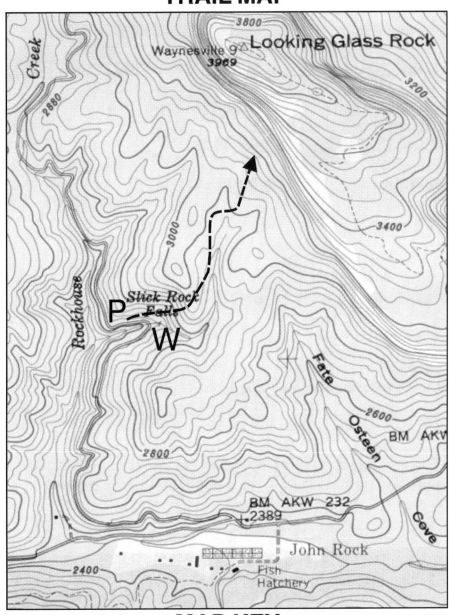

- 3800
- Wayneswile 9△ Looking Glass Rock
- 3969
- Creek
- 2880
- 3200
- 3400
- 3000
- Rockhouse
- Slick Rock Falls
- P
- W
- Fate
- 2600
- Osteen
- BM AKW
- 2800
- BM AKW 232
- 2389
- John Rock
- Cove
- 2400
- Fish Hatchery

MAP KEY

FEATURED HIKE	----▶	US ROUTE	
OTHER TRAILS	··········	STATE ROUTE	
PARKING	P	FOREST ROAD	
WATERFALLS	W	GATE	●━●

STAY ON THE TRAIL. DO NOT CUT SWITCHBACKS.

SUNWALL

TRAILHEAD:	SUNWALL PARKING AREA
TRAIL FINISH:	SUNWALL PARKING AREA
BLAZE COLOR:	YELLOW
HIKING DISTANCE:	0.8 MILE
DIFFICULTY:	MODERATE
TIME ALLOWANCE:	45 MINUTES
ELEVATION CHANGE:	420 FT.
USGS MAP:	SHINING ROCK

HIGHLIGHTS:

A nice hike up to the face of Looking Glass Rock and you might even see some climbers while you are there.

TRAIL DESCRIPTION:

- The parking area is tricky to find on forest road 475B but the trail is marked on the right hand side of the parking area.

- Follow the trail markers, difficult at the end.

- .4 mile you reach the rock face. Caution: Climbers may be on the rock, stay well out of their way.

- Follow the same trail back to the parking area.

PACK IT IN , PACK IT OUT.

TRAIL MAP

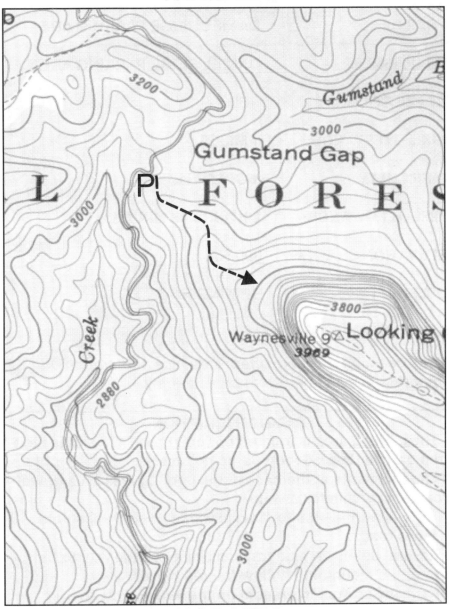

MAP KEY

FEATURED HIKE	---➤	US ROUTE
OTHER TRAILS	··············	STATE ROUTE
PARKING	P	FOREST ROAD
WATERFALLS	W	GATE

STAY ON THE TRAIL. DO NOT CUT SWITCHBACKS.

DANIEL RIDGE LOOP

TRAILHEAD:	DANIEL RIDGE PARKING AREA
TRAIL FINISH:	DANIEL RIDGE PARKING AREA
BLAZE COLOR:	RED
HIKING DISTANCE:	4 MILES
DIFFICULTY:	MODERATE
TIME ALLOWANCE:	2 HOURS 45 MINUTES
ELEVATION CHANGE:	800 FT.
USGS MAP:	SHINING ROCK

HIGHLIGHTS:

The stream on this hike offers very nice photographic opportunities and places to sit and enjoy.

TRAIL DESCRIPTION:

- The parking area is located on forest road 475 and is next to the Cove Creek Group Camping area.
- The trail starts at the back of the parking area on a gravel road, follow this for .2 mile.
- Turn left at the sign for Daniel Ridge Loop Trail, an old access road.
- Several unknown side trails intersect on the way to the top of the mountain. Follow the red blazes.
- Farlow Gap Trail intersects on the left. Follow the red blazes to the right.
- Approximately two-thirds of the way down is an intersection with a new logging road, not on the map. Straight across continue on the trail.
- Intersection with access road, turn right, follow this back to the parking area.

PACK IT IN , PACK IT OUT.

TRAIL MAP

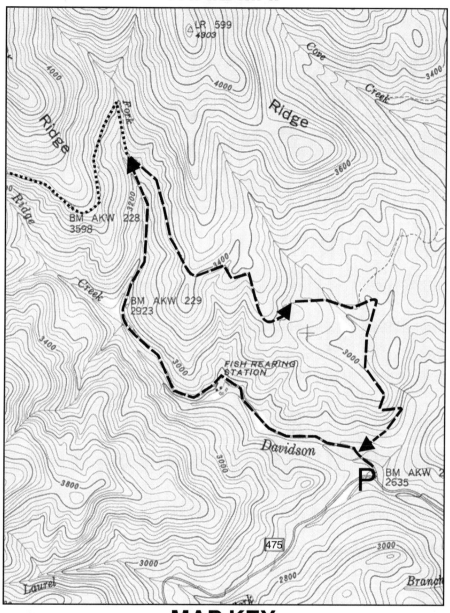

MAP KEY

FEATURED HIKE	▪▪▪▪▪➤	**US ROUTE**
OTHER TRAILS	▪▪▪▪▪▪▪▪▪▪	**STATE ROUTE**
PARKING	**P**	**FOREST ROAD**
WATERFALLS	**W**	**GATE**

STAY ON THE TRAIL. DO NOT CUT SWITCHBACKS.

PILOT COVE LOOP

TRAILHEAD:	PILOT COVE LOOP AND SLATE ROCK
TRAIL FINISH:	PILOT COVE LOOP AND SLATE ROCK
BLAZE COLOR:	YELLOW
HIKING DISTANCE:	3.6 MILES
DIFFICULTY:	MODERATE
TIME ALLOWANCE:	2 HOURS 30 MINUTES
ELEVATION CHANGE:	990 FT.
USGS MAP:	DUNSMORE MOUNTAIN

HIGHLIGHTS:

Pilot Cove Loop offers a diversity of terrain and an incredible view from an outcropping that overlooks the Pisgah Ranger District.

TRAIL DESCRIPTION:

- The small parking area is located off forest road 1206 and is marked with a sign for Slate Rock and Pilot Cove Loop.

- .2 mile Pilot Cove Loop, yellow blazes, on the right go straight on Slate Rock and Pilot Cove Loop, blue blazes.

- 1 mile is the ridgeline and Pilot Cove Loop is on your right, turn onto this trail.

- The trail runs on top of a rock. Caution: Rock cliffs can be dangerous or even fatal.

- At the bottom turn left back on Slate Rock and Pilot Cove Loop.

PACK IT IN , PACK IT OUT.

TRAIL MAP

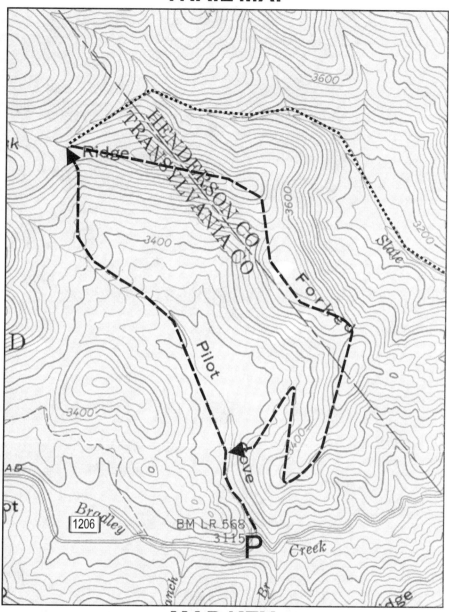

MAP KEY

FEATURED HIKE   - - - - ▶   US ROUTE

OTHER TRAILS   ··············   STATE ROUTE

PARKING   P   FOREST ROAD

WATERFALLS   W   GATE

STAY ON THE TRAIL. DO NOT CUT SWITCHBACKS.

South Fork Mills River

DIFFICULT HIKES

PRESSLEY COVE
COLD MOUNTAIN
BAD FORK
BENNETT GAP
WAGON ROAD GAP

PRESSLEY COVE

TRAILHEAD:	PRESSLEY COVE PARKING AREA
TRAIL FINISH:	PRESSLEY COVE PARKING AREA
BLAZE COLOR:	ORANGE
HIKING DISTANCE:	3.5 MILES
DIFFICULTY:	DIFFICULT
TIME ALLOWANCE:	2 HOURS 30 MINUTES
ELEVATION CHANGE:	950 FT.
USGS MAP:	PISGAH FOREST

HIGHLIGHTS:

Pressley Cove trail takes you up the mountain crossing back and forth over a small stream. At the top there are beautiful views from older clearcut areas.

TRAIL DESCRIPTION:

- The parking area is located immediately after the third bridge on forest road 477 if you are coming from the end near the ranger station.
- Across the road from the parking area the trail starts-- marked Pressley Cove. Do not take the trail that starts up the mountain immediately. Hike in the flat area parallel to the road until you reach the trees on the far side, that is where Pressley Cove turns up the mountain.
- 1.1 mile turn left on the logging road. Several old roads intersect; continue downhill and to the left at these inter- sections.
- When you reach the bottom on 477 turn left and follow this back to the parking area.

PACK IT IN , PACK IT OUT.

TRAIL MAP

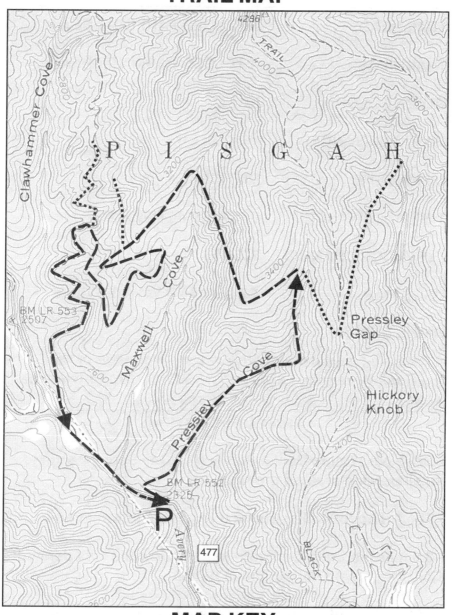

MAP KEY

FEATURED HIKE	- - - ▶	US ROUTE
OTHER TRAILS	·············	STATE ROUTE
PARKING	**P**	FOREST ROAD
WATERFALLS	**W**	GATE

STAY ON THE TRAIL. DO NOT CUT SWITCHBACKS.

COLD MOUNTAIN

TRAILHEAD:	**ART LOEB PARKING AREA**
TRAIL FINISH:	**ART LOEB PARKING AREA**
BLAZE COLOR:	**NONE**
HIKING DISTANCE:	**10.4 MILES**
DIFFICULTY:	**DIFFICULT**
TIME ALLOWANCE:	**6 HOURS 45 MINUTES**
ELEVATION CHANGE:	**2850 FT.**
USGS MAP:	**CRUSO AND WAYNESVILLE**

HIGHLIGHTS:

Incredible views from the top of Cold Mountain of the Shining Rock Wilderness Area and the Middle Prong Wilderness Area.

TRAIL DESCRIPTION:

- Drive past Camp Daniel Boone (the Boy Scout Camp) to a small parking area on the right.

- The Art Loeb Trail starts next to a large information board.

- 3.8 miles is Deep Gap, turn left.   Follow the well defined Cold Mountain Trail, up the mountain.

- At the ridge of the mountain there is a small camp site, turn right. Follow this on up to the top.

- Return back the same way you came up.

PACK IT IN , PACK IT OUT.

TRAIL MAP

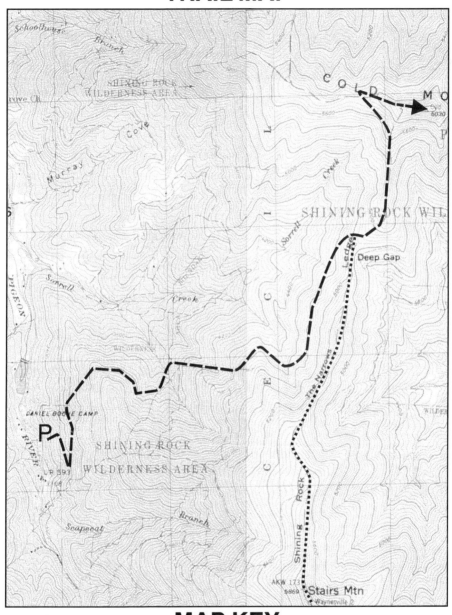

MAP KEY

FEATURED HIKE	---→	**US ROUTE**
OTHER TRAILS	··········	**STATE ROUTE**
PARKING	**P**	**FOREST ROAD**
WATERFALLS	**W**	**GATE**

STAY ON THE TRAIL. DO NOT CUT SWITCHBACKS.

BAD FORK

TRAILHEAD:	BAD FORK PARKING AREA
TRAIL FINISH:	BAD FORK PARKING AREA
BLAZE COLOR:	ORANGE
HIKING DISTANCE:	4 MILES
DIFFICULTY:	DIFFICULT
TIME ALLOWANCE:	2 HOURS 30 MINUTES
ELEVATION CHANGE:	700 FT.
USGS MAP:	DUNSMORE MOUNTAIN

HIGHLIGHTS:

Bad Fork is an interesting trail with several bridged creek crossings and it basically runs right up the mountain. Nice views in the fall and winter with the absence of foliage.

TRAIL DESCRIPTION:

- The trail is located across from a large field which is a designated roadside camping area on Wash Creek Road, forest road 5000.

- The trail head marker was not present. However, the trail was marked with an orange blaze that is visible from the road.

- 2 miles the trail ends on the forest road next to the Blue Ridge Parkway. Very steep sections near the end.

- Turn back down the trail and follow it back to the parking area.

PACK IT IN , PACK IT OUT.

TRAIL MAP

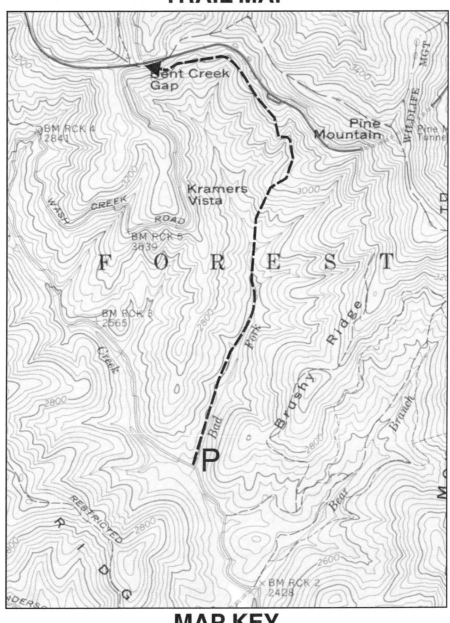

MAP KEY

FEATURED HIKE	------▶	US ROUTE	
OTHER TRAILS	·············	STATE ROUTE	
PARKING	**P**	FOREST ROAD	
WATERFALLS	**W**	GATE	•——•

STAY ON THE TRAIL. DO NOT CUT SWITCHBACKS.

BENNETT GAP

TRAILHEAD:	BENNETT GAP PARKING AREA
TRAIL FINISH:	BENNETT GAP PARKING AREA
BLAZE COLOR:	RED
HIKING DISTANCE:	4.3 MILES
DIFFICULTY:	DIFFICULT
TIME ALLOWANCE:	3 HOURS 30 MINUTES
ELEVATION CHANGE:	1290 FT.
USGS MAP:	SHINING ROCK, PISGAH FOREST

HIGHLIGHTS:

Open vistas of Looking Glass Rock, high fields with views, hardwood forests, rhododendron tunnels, creeks and streams.

TRAIL DESCRIPTION:
- Parking area located near the top of forest road 477.
- Trail starts across the road from the parking area and is marked as Bennett Gap Trail.
- .8 mile Perry Cove connects to the left, stay straight.
- 1.0 mile Coontree Loop connects to the right, stay straight.
- 1.4 miles Coontree Loop separates from Bennet Gap on the right, stay straight.
- 1.9 miles Bennett Gap ends on forest road 477, turn left. Caution: Motor vehicle traffic.
- Go past the horse stables on right, cross bridge and turn left at next gated road.
- 2.3 miles Perry Cove Trail, on right, orange blazes.
- 3.5 miles turn right on Bennett Gap.
- Follow Bennett Gap back to parking area.

PACK IT IN , PACK IT OUT.

TRAIL MAP

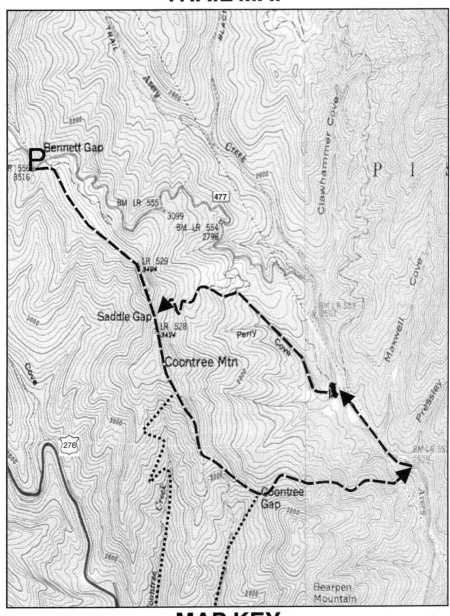

MAP KEY

FEATURED HIKE	- - - ▶	US ROUTE
OTHER TRAILS	··············	STATE ROUTE
PARKING	**P**	FOREST ROAD
WATERFALLS	**W**	GATE

STAY ON THE TRAIL. DO NOT CUT SWITCHBACKS.

WAGON ROAD GAP

TRAILHEAD:	TURKEYPEN TRAIL HEAD
TRAIL FINISH:	TURKEYPEN TRAIL HEAD
BLAZE COLOR:	ORANGE
HIKING DISTANCE:	5 MILES
DIFFICULTY:	DIFFICULT
TIME ALLOWANCE:	3 HOURS 30 MINUTES
ELEVATION CHANGE:	1330 FT.
USGS MAP:	PISGAH FOREST

HIGHLIGHTS:

A wide diversity of terrain from the ridgeline to the river captures the broad spectrum of hiking in the Pisgah Ranger District.

TRAIL DESCRIPTION:
- The trail head is located on Turkeypen Road off 280 near the Henderson Co. and Transylvania Co. line. Follow the gravel road to the parking area.
- Start on Turkey Pen Gap Trail, located between the horse trailer parking area and the car parking area.
- Steep climb over Sharpy Mtn. and through several saddles is Wagon Road Gap, trail on the right. Not marked but there is trail definition that runs down from the saddle.
- At the bottom of the mountain turn right on S. Mills River.
- Go across the river on the swinging bridge, right turn after crossing.
- Hard right off the access road to cross another swinging bridge.
- Turn right after the swinging bridge.
- Follow this up the mountain and back to the parking area.

PACK IT IN , PACK IT OUT.

TRAIL MAP

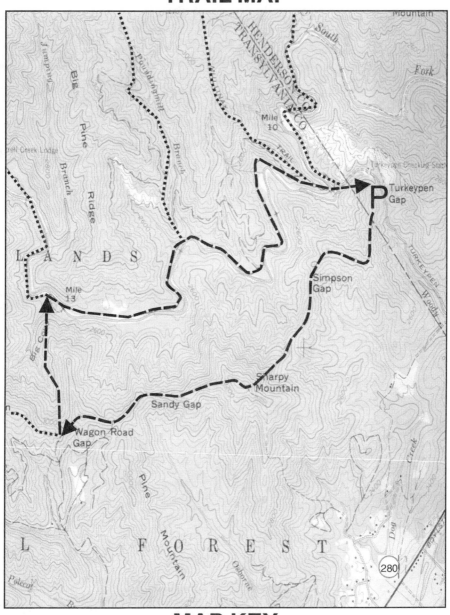

MAP KEY

FEATURED HIKE   ------▶   US ROUTE

OTHER TRAILS   ••••••••••••   STATE ROUTE

PARKING   **P**   FOREST ROAD

WATERFALLS   **W**   GATE

STAY ON THE TRAIL. DO NOT CUT SWITCHBACKS.

Looking Glass Falls

REGIONAL
INFORMATION
AND
POINTS OF INTEREST

NATIONAL FOREST CAMPGROUNDS

DAVIDSON RIVER

Located off US 276 near Brevard.
161 Sites
Fee: $13.00 + reservation fee
Showers available
Restrooms available
Firewood available
One loop open year-round
Reservations for some sites
Reservation number (800) 280-2267
Maximum stay 14 days
Davidson River offers a variety of activities
in the heart of the Pisgah Ranger District
e.g. fishing, mountain biking, horseback
riding and rock climbing.

LAKE POWHATAN

Located off 191 near Asheville.
98 Sites
Fee: $12.00 + reservation fee
Showers available
Restrooms available
Firewood available
Open April 1 - October 30
Reservation number (800) 280-2267
Maximum stay 14 days
Lake Powhatan activities include swimming,
fishing, horseback riding, mountain biking and a
short hike to the NC Arboretum.

NORTH MILLS RIVER

Located approximately halfway between
Asheville and Brevard off 280.
31 Sites
Fee: $6.00 + reservation fee
No showers
Restrooms available
No firewood
Open April 1 - November 15
Reservations for some sites
Reservation number (800) 280-2267
Maximum stay 14 days
North Mills River offers fishing, mountain
        biking, and horseback riding.

SUNBURST

Located off 215 near Waynesville.
10 Sites
Fee: $5.00
No showers
Restrooms available
No firewood
Open April 1 - December 30
No reservations
Maximum stay 14 days
Sunburst activities include fishing and the
        wilderness area for exploring.

Additional information about the Pisgah Ranger District camp-
grounds can be obtained by contacting the Ranger Station.

District Ranger
USDA Forest Service
1001 Pisgah Hwy.
Pisgah Forest, NC 28768
(828) 877-3265

PRIVATE CAMPGROUNDS

BREVARD

BLACK FOREST FAMILY CAMPING RESORT
90 sites, 21 full hook-ups, cabins
Fees: 2 persons $16 tents, $20-$22 RV's, $30-$40 cabins
Open March 15 - December 1
Phone # (828) 884-2267
Showers, restrooms, firewood, fire rings, and laundry available
Activities: Swimming pool, playground, horseshoes, hiking trails,
    badminton.

ASHEVILLE

THE FRENCH BROAD RIVER CAMPGROUND
44 sites, 10 full hook-ups
Fees: 4 persons $15-$20
Open year round
Phone # (828) 658-0772
Showers, restrooms, firewood, laundry, phones
Activities: Canoeing, fishing, horseshoes, volleyball, kayak and
    tube rentals.

BALSAM

MOONSHINE CREEK CAMPGROUND
92 sites, 50 full hook-ups, cabins
Fees: 2 persons $19-$24, cabins vary
Open April 1 - November 1
Phone # (828) 586-6666
Showers, restrooms, firewood, laundry, phones
Activities: Fishing, horseshoes, hiking, volleyball.

CANTON

BIG COVE CAMPGROUND
63 sites, 21 full hook-ups, cabins
Fees: 2 persons $10 tents, $15-$18 RV's, $15 cabins
Open year round
Phone # (828) 667-9376
Showers, restrooms, firewood, laundry, phones
Activities: Swimming pool, horseback riding, playground, horse
        shoes, hiking trails.

HENDERSONVILLE

RED GATES RV PARK
18 sites,14 full hook-up, cabins
Fees: 2 persons $10
Open April 1 - November 1
Phone # (828) 685-8787
Showers, restrooms, laundry
Activites: Swimming, boating, boat rentals, fishing, basketball,
        shuffle board.

BLUE RIDGE PARKWAY

THE PISGAH INN AND CAMPGROUND
137 sites, no hook-ups
Fees: campground 2 persons $12; Inn $70, $78, $110
Open April - November
Phone # (828) 235 -8228
For camping there are bathrooms but no showers.
Centrally located in Pisgah Ranger District.

OTHER TYPES OF CAMPING

PRIMITIVE CAMPING

Generally speaking this is what most people consider backpacking. Carrying essential items into the backcountry away from running water, toilets etc., for the experience of being away from civilization. This is not for the faint of heart or the bungling idiot to take upon themselves. It takes careful planning, understanding the area that you will be going into, and how to behave as a low impact camper. There are hundreds of books on the subject; a few are listed in the recommended reading section of this book. Other good sources of information are your local outdoor retailer, magazines that cover backpacking and the district office.

Special considerations for primitive camping in the Pisgah Ranger District are camping at least 1/4 mile from any road that is open for vehicle use, sanitary disposal of human waste, no washing in streams or creeks; or cutting of live trees, shrubs, or bushes for firewood. As always in any camping situation please clean up after yourself, carry out all trash that you have brought and the trash anyone may have left. The next people that come to your camp will thank you. Some other considerations are the designated wilderness areas, where group size is limited to 10 persons and campfires are forbidden.

ROADSIDE CAMPING

Permitted in areas that are posted with a sign shown below. Vehicles must be in the area provided and cannot block traffic or gates. Persons are required to clean up the camp before leaving and dispose of human waste in a sanitary manner. Persons cannot cut firewood or wash in the streams and creeks. Length of stay cannot exceed 14 days.

POINTS OF INTEREST

THE FOREST DISCOVERY CENTER
Located at the Cradle of Forestry in America on US 276 and is where forestry education got its start.
Activities: Guided tours, exhibits, historic buildings, and gift shop.
Fees: $4.00 adults, $2.00 young adults, under 6 free.
Open April - October : 9am to 5pm

SLIDING ROCK
A natural rock waterslide on US 276.
Activities: Observation and participation in sliding on the rock.
Fees: $3.00 per vehicle or $1.00 per person-group rate
Open end of May - mid August
Restrooms, changing areas

LOOKING GLASS FALLS
Freefalling 60 foot waterfall on US 276.
Fees: none
Roadside parking

FISH HATCHERY
Trout hatchery on forest service road 475.
Activities: Observing the various trout species.
Fees: none
No facilities

BLUE RIDGE PARKWAY
A two lane scenic road that travels out of Asheville to Cherokee and traverses the Pisgah National Forest. Many beautiful over-looks that give stunning views of the national forest.
Some sections may be closed in the winter due to ice and snow.

LAKE POWHATAN
A beautiful lake to swim in and beach area with picnic tables.
Fee: $3.00 per car
Open April 1 - October 30 10:00 am to sunset.

CHAMBERS OF COMMERCE

The area chambers of commerce hold a wealth of information to visitors and newcomers. They can tell you of upcoming events, places to stay, festivals, businesses, and other things that may be of interest to you. It is beyond the scope of this book to begin to list such items. I strongly recommend that you contact them and find out what is happening at the time of your visit.

ASHEVILLE AREA CHAMBER OF COMMERCE
151 Haywood St.
Asheville, NC 28801
(800) 257-5583
www.ashevillechamber.org

BLACK MOUNTAIN CHAMBER OF COMMERCE
201 E. State St.
Black Mountain, NC 28711-3597
(828) 669-2300

BREVARD CHAMBER OF COMMERCE
35 W. Main St.
Brevard, NC 28712-3633
(828) 883-3700

CASHIERS AREA CHAMBER OF COMMERCE
HWY 107 N.
Cashiers, NC 28717
(828) 743-5191

CHEROKEE TRAVEL & PROMOTION
Main St.
Cherokee, NC 28719-2754
(828) 497-9195

FRANKLIN AREA CHAMBER OF COMMERCE
Linda Harbuck
425 Porter St.

Franklin, NC 28734
(828) 524-3161
www.franklin-chamber.com

GREATER HENDERSONVILLE CHAMBER OF COMMERCE
330 North King St.
Hendersonville, NC 28792
(828) 692-1413
www.hendersonvillenc.org

HAYWOOD COUNTY CHAMBER OF COMMERCE
Tom Knapko or Melanie Cutshaw
PO Drawer 600
Waynesville, NC 28786
(828) 456-3021
www.haywood-nc.com

HIGHLANDS CHAMBER OF COMMERCE
396 Oak St.
Highlands, NC 28779-5412
(828) 526-2112

JACKSON COUNTY CHAMBER OF COMMERCE
116 Central St.
Sylva, NC 28779
(828) 586-2155
www.nc-mountains.com

SWAIN COUNTY CHAMBER OF COMMERCE
Richard Schaddelee
PO Box 509
Bryson City, NC 28713
(800) 867-9246
www.greatsmokies.com

LOCAL OUTDOOR RETAILERS

NAPLES
DIAMOND BRAND CAMPING CENTER
(828) 684-6262

ASHEVILLE
BLACK DOME MOUNTAIN SPORTS
(828) 251-2001

B. B. BARNES
(828) 274-7301

HENDERSONVILLE
MAST GENERAL STORE
(828) 696-1883

WAYNESVILLE
MAST GENERAL STORE
(828) 452-2101

BREVARD
LOOKING GLASS OUTFITTERS
(828) 884-5854

BACKCOUNTRY OUTDOORS
(828) 883-9453

DILLSBORO
VENTURE OUT
(828) 586-1464

BLACK MOUNTAIN
BLUE SPRUCE OUTFITTERS
(828) 669-6965

FRANKLIN
THREE EAGLES OUTFITTERS AND GALLERY
(828) 524-9061

CHEROKEE
QUEENS TRADING POST & OUTFITTERS
(828) 497-4453

HIGHLANDS
HIGHLAND HIKER
(828) 743-1732

BRYSON CITY
NANTAHALA OUTDOOR CENTER
(828) 488-2446

WESSER
NANTAHALA OUTDOOR CENTER
(800) 367-3521

BOONE
MAST GENERAL STORE
(828) 262-0000

FOOTSLOGGER'S
(828) 262-5111

RALEIGH
GREAT OUTDOOR PROVISIONS COMPANY
(919) 833-1741

TRAVELERS REST, SC
SUNRIFT ADVENTURES
(803) 834-3019

RECOMMENDED READING

GENERAL HIKING

THE COMPLETE WALKER III
by Colin Fletcher
published by Alfred A. Knopf
ISBN 0-394-72264-7

THE DAYHIKER'S HANDBOOK
by John Long and Michael Hodgson
published by Ragged Mountain Press
ISBN 0-07-029146-2

HIKING & BACKPACKING:
a complete guide
by Karen Berger
a Trailside series guide
published by W. W. Norton & Company
ISBN 0-393-31334-4

WALKING SOFTLY IN THE WILDERNESS
by John Hart
The Sierra Club Guide to Backpacking
published by Sierra Club Books
ISBN 0-07156-813-6

MINIMUM IMPACT HIKING & CAMPING

SOFT PATHS
by Bruce Hampton and David Cole
a NOLS guide
published by Stackpole Books
ISBN 0-8117-2234-1

FIRST AID

NOLS Wilderness First Aid
by Tod Schimelpfenig and Linda Lindsey
published by Stackpole Books
ISBN 0-8117-3084-0

NORTH CAROLINA HIKING TRAILS
by Allen de Hart
published by the Appalachian Mountain Club
ISBN 1-878239-48-1

NORTH CAROLINA
A Guide to Backcountry Travel & Adventure
by James Bannon
published by out there press
ISBN 0-9648584-0-1

HIGHROAD GUIDE TO THE
NORTH CAROLINA MOUNTAINS
by Lynda McDaniel
published by Longstreet Press, Inc.
ISBN 1-56352-463-5

FIELD GUIDES
THE PETERSON FIELD GUIDE SERIES
published by Houghton Mifflin Company

THE NATIONAL AUDUBON SOCIETY FIELD GUIDES
published by Afred A. Knopf, Inc.

MAPS
PISGAH RANGER DISTRICT
North Carolina
published by Trails Illustrated

PISGAH DISTRICT TRAIL MAP
Pisgah National Forest North Carolina
published by the Cradle of Forestry in America Interpretive
Association

ENVIRONMENTAL ORGANIZATIONS AND HIKING GROUPS

AMERICAN HIKING SOCIETY
PO Box 20160
Washington, DC 20041-2160
(301) 565-6704
www.americanhiking.org

APPALACHIAN TRAIL CONFERENCE
PO Box 807
Harper's Ferry, WV 25425
(304) 535-6331

CAROLINA MOUNTAIN CLUB
John Pawcio
PO Box 68
Asheville, NC 28802
(828) 299-8126

ENVIRONMENTAL DEFENSE FUND
1875 Connecticut Ave. Northwest
Washington, DC 20009
(202) 387-3525
members@edf.org

FRIENDS OF STATE PARKS
4204 Randleman Rd.
Greensboro, NC 27406

FRIENDS OF THE BLUE RIDGE PARKWAY
Susan J. Mills, PhD
PO Box 341
Arden, NC 28704
(828) 687-8722
usfriends@aol.com

NC WILDLIFE FEDERATION
PO Box 10626
Raleigh, NC 27605
(919) 833-1923

NATIONAL AUDUBON SOCIETY
700 Broadway
New York, NY 10003

THE NATURE CONSERVANCY
4245 North Fairfax Dr. Suite 100
Arlington, VA 22203-1606
(703) 841-5300
www.tnc.org

RAILS-TO-TRAILS CONSERVANCY
1100 17th St., Northwest Fl. 10
Washington, DC 20036
(202) 331-9696

SIERRA CLUB
85 2nd St. Fl. 2
San Francisco, CA 94105
(415) 977-5500

THE SOUTHERN APPALACHIAN HIGHLANDS CONSER-VANCY
Kristy Urquhart
34 Wall St., Suite 802
Asheville, NC 28801-2710
(828) 253-0095
southapps@ioa.com

THE WILDERNESS SOCIETY
Shirl Parsons
1447 Peachtree St., Northeast Ste. 812
Atlanta, GA 30309-3029
(404) 872-9453

GPS UTM WAYPOINTS

Art Loeb parking area	17 S	0327800
		3917400
Bad Fork parking area	17 S	0349600
		3922000
Bear Branch parking area	17 S	0349900
		3921300
Bennett Gap parking area	17 S	0338600
		3909950
Black Balsam parking area	17 S	0328900
		3910600
Buck Spring parking area	17 S	0338200
		3915200
Cold Mountain	17 S	0331400
		3919900
Coontree picnic area	17 S	0339700
		3906400
Courthouse Falls parking area	17 S	0327900
		3904800
Daniel Ridge parking area	17 S	0333700
		3905900
Davidson River Campground	17 S	0343300
		3905400
Devil's Courthouse parking area	17 S	0327400
		3908300
Fish Hatchery parking area	17 S	0337100
		3905800
Graveyard Fields parking area	17 S	0332300
		3909900
Long Branch parking area	17 S	0332500
		3904700
Looking Glass Rock parking area	17 S	0338400
		3906600
Moore Cove parking area	17 S	0338600
		3907950
Mount Pisgah	17 S	0340500
		3921400

Mount Pisgah parking area	17 S	0341300
		3920600
North Mills River Campground	17 S	0350500
		3919200
Pilot Cove parking area	17 S	0344200
		3916700
Pink Beds parking area	17 S	0338300
		3913400
Pisgah Ranger Station	17 S	0342900
		3905800
Pressley Cove parking area	17 S	0341800
		3908100
Slick Rock Falls parking area	17 S	0336500
		3906800
Sunwall parking area	17 S	0336300
		3908600
Thompson Creek parking area	17 S	0341500
		3916600
Turkey Pen trail head	17 S	0349200
		3912100

Handheld GPS units are interesting and fun for anyone who enjoys the outdoors. Unfortunately, they have certain limitations in accuracy due to the error the government intentionally puts in the signals from the satellites. Because of this error you shouldn't use a GPS as your only source of navigation; a map and compass are still necessities to carry on your hikes and know how to use. These GPS waypoints have been added as a fun reference for the many people who own GPS units. These points are not the exact locations of the parking area or trail head and have been rounded to the nearest 100 meters. Use them to find the general location of your parking area or to find how far it is to the top of the mountain.

NOTES

UPDATE FORM

MAILING INFORMATION:

NAME:
ADDRESS:

PHONE NUMBER: E-MAIL:

INDIVIDUAL INFORMATION:

AGE: GENDER:
UNDER 20   M   F
20 TO 29
30 TO 39   HOW MANY TIMES/
40 TO 49   YR. DO YOU HIKE?
50 TO 59   1 TO 5
OVER 60   6 TO 15
                                        16 TO 25
HIKING EXPERIENCE: OVER 26
BEGINNER
INTERMEDIATE   HOW DID YOU
ADVANCED   LEARN OF THIS
                                        PUBLICATION?
OTHER INTERESTS: LOCAL RETAILER
BACKPACKING   FRIEND/FAMILY
MOUNTAIN BIKING   BOOKSTORE
HORSEBACK RIDING   OTHER _____
ROAD BIKING
CANOEING/KAYAKING
RUNNING
OTHER_____

Please Return To:
Soco Publishing
Attn: Kirk Edwards
PO BOX 1021
Sylva, NC 28779-1021

QUESTIONS AND COMMENTS

UPDATE FORM

MAILING INFORMATION:

NAME:
ADDRESS:

PHONE NUMBER: **E-MAIL:**

INDIVIDUAL INFORMATION:

AGE: **GENDER:**
UNDER 20   M   F
20 TO 29
30 TO 39   **HOW MANY TIMES/**
40 TO 49   **YR. DO YOU HIKE?**
50 TO 59   1 TO 5
OVER 60   6 TO 15
                                     16 TO 25
HIKING EXPERIENCE: OVER 26
BEGINNER
INTERMEDIATE   **HOW DID YOU**
ADVANCED   **LEARN OF THIS**
                                     PUBLICATION?
OTHER INTERESTS: **LOCAL RETAILER**
BACKPACKING   **FRIEND/FAMILY**
MOUNTAIN BIKING   **BOOKSTORE**
HORSEBACK RIDING   OTHER _____
ROAD BIKING
CANOEING/KAYAKING
RUNNING
OTHER_____

Please Return To:
Soco Publishing
Attn: Kirk Edwards
PO BOX 1021
Sylva, NC 28779-1021

QUESTIONS AND COMMENTS

ORDER FORM

Please patronize your local outdoor retailer and bookstore.

The following prices are subject to change.

Hiking North Carolina's Pisgah Ranger District
published by Soco Publishing
ISBN 0-9668870-0-X $14.95   QTY. _____

Hiking North Carolina's Pisgah Ranger District and
Trails Illustrated Map Set
ISBN 0-9668870-1-8 $21.95   QTY. _____

Pisgah Ranger District North Carolina
published by Trails Illustrated
ISBN 0-925873-87-X $8.99   QTY. _____

COMING SOON FROM SOCO PUBLISHING

Flat Water Paddling In Western North Carolina

Hiking North Carolina's Nantahala National Forest

Please send information when published.   [ ]

OVER

Shipping and handling is $3.50 for the first book and $.50 for each additional book.

Prices are subject to change.

Return shipment to:
Please print

Name

Address

Phone Number

Bill me later or
send check or money order and this page to:

Soco Publishing
PO Box 1021
Sylva, NC 28779-1021

Thank you for your order.